Grampa and the Ghost

SHIRLEY-RAYE REDMOND began freelance writing while living in Lincoln, Illinois—*without* the assistance of a "ghost"! She now lives in Los Alamos, New Mexico, with her husband Bill and their youngsters, Bethany and Jordan. This is her first book for children.

Grampa and the Ghost

SHIRLEY-RAYE REDMOND

AN AVON CAMELOT BOOK

GRAMPA AND THE GHOST is an original publication of Avon Books. This work has never before appeared in book form.

AVON BOOKS
A division of
The Hearst Corporation
1350 Avenue of the Americas
New York, New York 10019

Published by arrangement with the author
Library of Congress Catalog Card Number: 93-90666
ISBN: 0-380-77382-1
RL: 3.8

First Avon Camelot Printing: April 1994

Printed in the U.S.A.

OPM 10 9 8 7 6 5 4 3 2 1

Dedicated with love
to
Binky, Toot, and Kiki

CONTENTS

One
WANTED: ONE GHOST
1

Two
THE GHOSTLY VISITOR
11

Three
THE POSITION IS FILLED
17

Four
DOUBTFUL THOUGHTS
29

Five
TALLULAH IN CHARGE
39

Six
GRAMPA TAKES CARE OF EVERYTHING
49

Seven
PROBLEMS
57

Eight
SOLUTIONS!
63

Nine
A HOME FOR TALLULAH
73

Grampa and the Ghost

One

WANTED: ONE GHOST

When Mark finished writing the ad for the newspaper, it read:

> Wanted: Professional ghost to help write autobiographical adventure story. Contact W. Gaffney, 123 Pekin Street, Lincoln, IL

Had he known what problems these simple words would cause, ten-year-old Mark might have dropped the whole idea of advertising for a ghostwriter in the first place. But he didn't know. Unaware of the astonishing events that would soon take place, Mark read the words out loud to his sister and his grandfather.

"Sounds okay to me," Sibyl declared, "real businesslike."

"I don't believe it!" Mark exclaimed in mock surprise. "Sibling approves!"

Sibyl wrinkled up her nose at him. She hated being called "sibling" and Mark knew it. Ever since she had turned nine, Sibyl did not want to be reminded that she was Mark's younger sister. In fact, she wanted to forget that they were related at all. But one look at their fuzzy brown hair, their heavy eyebrows, and their freckled faces and anyone could tell that Mark and Sibyl were brother and sister.

"Well, what do you think of it, Grampa?" Mark asked. He turned to the elderly man who sat at the end of the small kitchen table. Grampa was slowly stirring sugar into his mug of coffee. His gray hair, or what was left of it, had not been combed. His sweater was missing a button and needed to be washed. "Does it sound okay to you?"

"Grumpff!" replied Grampa Will. This was his usual response to anything he hadn't made up his mind about yet. It sounded like he was snorting and clearing his throat at the same time.

"What's a fuss-and-shell ghost?" Jeremy asked, tilting his blond head to one side. He was only three.

"The word is 'pro-fes-sion-al.' " Mark pronounced the word carefully.

"That's what he said!" Sibyl insisted, putting her arm around her small brother's shoulders. Jeremy stood by her chair and waited, with wide-open eyes, for Mark to answer his question.

"A professional ghost is a writer who writes stories for people who don't know how," Mark explained. Their dad was an English teacher, so Mark and Sibyl had learned many interesting things about writing.

"But Grampa knows how to write!" Jeremy protested. "Don't you, Grampa?"

"Grumpff!" the man replied.

"Well, sure Grampa can write," Mark amended, "but he wants to write a book." He watched Sibyl pluck the lint off Jeremy's red corduroy overalls. Mark grinned. His sister reminded him of a mother monkey he'd seen once at the zoo picking fleas from her baby's fur.

"But why does a ghost have to write Grampa's book?" Jeremy asked his smirking brother. "Is it going to be a ghost story? A scary one?"

Sibyl chuckled softly and murmured, "Silly beans!" affectionately into Jeremy's ear. Grampa Will grinned. His face crinkled into dozens of wrinkly creases.

"No, Jeremy, it's not going to be a ghost story," Grampa Will said. His gray, watery eyes glinted with good humor. He sipped his coffee. "It's going to be a true-life adventure story," he told him. "A long time ago, before I married your Nana Rosa, I once helped a missionary doctor build a small hospital out in the middle of the African jungle. I had quite a time when I was there!" Grampa said. His eyes were shining with a reminiscent glimmer.

"I hunted elephants and took a canoe trip on a river full of crocodiles. Once, I even had to jump out of bed in the middle of the night when my cabin was overrun by killer ants."

Jeremy was clearly fascinated, but Mark was not. He recognized the glint in his grandfather's eyes. He knew that once the man got started on his African adventure stories, he would go on forever. He interrupted Grampa Will impatiently. "Do I put the ad in the paper or not?" he asked.

Mark didn't mean to be rude, but he had heard these tales a thousand times. That was one of the reasons Mark wanted his grandfather to write a book—to get those stories out of his system. Besides, he and Sibyl agreed (and that was rare!) that Grampa Will needed something to do. Ever since Nana Rosa had died almost two years ago, Grampa had been very sad and depressed. He often forgot to take his blood pressure medicine. Sometimes he wouldn't change his clothes for several days, and he seemed to live on coffee and junk food.

That's why the family had persuaded Grampa Will to move into the converted coach house—the Little House, they called it—right behind the large blue one where Mark, Sibyl, and Jeremy lived with their parents, two goldfish, and a huge, lazy yellow cat named Hoodwink. The youngsters' father could now keep a closer eye on his dad, making sure that the elderly man took his medication and ate proper meals.

But still, Grampa had very little to do. That's why Mark had suggested that his grandfather write a book. "I'm no writer," Grampa had growled.

"What you need is a ghostwriter," Mark had suggested.

Sibyl had agreed enthusiastically. "You can tell your story to him, and he'll put it down on paper for you. He'll give your book a real professional touch," she added.

"So, what do you say, Grampa?" Mark asked again after presenting the suggested newspaper ad to his grandfather. "Shall I call and have this run in the paper?"

"Say yes!" Sibyl urged.

"I want the ghost to come! I want the ghost to come!" Jeremy chanted as he bounced up and down on Sibyl's lap.

"If a job's worth doing, it's worth doing right the first time," Mark reminded him. "That's what Nana Rosa always used to say."

Grampa Will pushed his chair away from the table. He ran a wrinkled hand through his messed-up hair. He shuffled over to the sink to rinse out his coffee mug. Watching him, Sibyl and Mark found it hard to believe that this was the same man who had once trekked through the dense jungles hunting elephants. Grampa seemed so frail and so old now. He needed to be protected.

"Maybe I ought to speak with your dad first," Grampa mumbled.

"Oh, no!" Sibyl exclaimed. "You can tell Mom and Dad all about it *after* you hire the ghostwriter."

"That's right," Mark agreed. "Tell them later on. But I need to know about the ad *now*. Should I put in anything else or is it okay the way it is?"

"Well, there is one thing," Grampa Will admitted hesitantly. "Put in there that I want a good speller."

"A good speller?" Sibyl asked with surprise.

"Grampa, there are dictionaries and—" Mark began, but his grandfather interrupted him.

"No. I want the writer to be able to spell. I don't want some fool asking me every five minutes how to spell one word or another."

"All right," Mark agreed reluctantly. He zipped up his coat and prepared to leave. "I'll add the part about the spelling."

Sibyl gently pushed her little brother off her lap. "Grampa wants a really good speller," Jeremy spoke up. "Don't ya, Grampa?"

"An excellent speller," Sibyl suggested.

"Put in 'exceptional speller,'" Grampa Will said with a note of decision in his tone. Mark nodded and then returned with Sibyl and Jeremy to the Big House. Before leaving for school, Mark furtively phoned the newspaper office and read the final version of the ad to the friendly female voice on the other end of the line:

> PROFESSIONAL GHOST WANTED to help write autobiographical adventure story. Must be an exceptional speller. Contact W. Gaffney, 123 Pekin Street, Lincoln, IL. (217) 555-1997

But their secret didn't remain one for long. Mr. Gaffney saw the ad in the paper later that evening. "I want to see you both in my study—*now!*" he said angrily, stomping into the kitchen.

Sibyl and Mark were doing their homework at the kitchen table. They exchanged nervous glances before slowly pushing back their chairs. Mrs. Gaffney, vigorously stirring some lumpy muffin batter, raised her eyebrows at them. But she didn't say a word as they left the kitchen and followed their father down the hall.

"I know that you two talked your grandfather into this," Mr. Gaffney said sternly. He circled the classified ad with a pencil. "And I think it's a waste of time and money. First of all, I doubt seriously that there are any professional ghostwriters—legitimate ones—in town. Second of all, the fees will be very expensive. Your grandfather—*if* he hires a professional writer, *if* one even applies for the job—will end up spending a lot of money on something that *should be* just an enjoyable pastime."

Mr. Gaffney frowned at his two oldest children and dropped his glasses onto the desk with a careless *plunk*. "What am I going to do with you two stooges?" he asked wearily, shaking his head.

"We *did* talk Grampa into putting the ad in the paper," Mark admitted. There was no use lying about it, he thought to himself. "And I told them to run it for three days. I'm paying for it with my allowance. I really think Grampa's African stories would make a great book, Dad.

But he needs someone with good writing skills to make it work out."

"Yes, and someone who can, er, spell," Mr. Gaffney commented with a wry smile, again pointing to the newspaper ad. Suddenly, his smile broadened into a grin.

Sibyl and Mark smiled sheepishly at one another. "*That* was Grampa's idea," Sibyl quickly pointed out.

"I only hope your grandfather won't have cause to regret this foolishness," Mr. Gaffney said, shaking his head slowly.

"What do you mean, Dad?" Sibyl asked. Her grin dissolved into a frown. "Why would Grampa Will be sorry about the ad?"

"You never can tell," her father replied vaguely. "He may be bothered by crank telephone calls or something worse, like a con artist."

"Gee, I never thought of that," Mark said, looking at his sister uneasily.

"No, I suppose you didn't," Mr. Gaffney replied with a worried sigh. "If your grandfather does get any calls about this ad, and if he wants to interview an applicant, promise me that you'll let me know so that I can check things out first."

"Yeah, sure!" Sibyl and Mark promised in unison.

"Maybe I ought to put a word of caution in your grandfather's ear," Mr. Gaffney murmured. He was staring down at the folded newspaper and tapping the page with his pencil.

"Maybe you'd better," Mark agreed.

"We sure don't want anything bad to happen to Grampa," Sibyl said, with a worried frown.

"No, of course you don't," their dad said, looking first at Sibyl and then at Mark. He smiled at them understandingly. "None of us do."

"We didn't mean to cause any trouble," Mark added with a shrug.

Mr. Gaffney simply nodded. "I know, I know," he said wearily. "Let's not worry about it now. It's nearly time for supper."

But neither Mark nor Sibyl felt much like eating. Could one little paragraph in the local newspaper really cause so much trouble?

Two

THE GHOSTLY VISITOR

The next day at school classes dragged. Sibyl was unable to concentrate on anything, not even math, which was her favorite subject. Instead, she simmered with curiosity all day long. Mark was ordinarily thankful that he rarely saw his sister at school. But today he was so anxious about someone answering the newspaper ad that he actually found himself wishing Sibyl could sit with him in the cafeteria.

Sibyl was the first one home after school. Along the way she noted that the snow in the front yards she passed was slushier than the day before. Patches of deep, chocolate-colored mud reminded Sibyl that spring was coming, and she could hardly wait.

Much to her dismay, however, Sibyl learned that they hadn't received a single inquiry about the ghostwriter's job. Mark, too, was disappointed when he came bursting through his grandfather's front door fifteen minutes later. He had an expectant look on his face. "Maybe Dad was right," Mark said. "Maybe it was just a waste of money to advertise for a ghostwriter."

The next evening when Grampa came over to have lasagna with the family, he admitted that he still had not had any calls about the ad. The youngsters gave up hope. "Perhaps I could have the ad run for a few more days," Grampa suggested. But there was no enthusiasm in his voice.

"Why bother, Dad?" Mr. Gaffney asked. "I've spoken with the head of the English department, and she's given me the names of two or three top-notch students. They would jump at the chance to help you with your book."

Mr. Gaffney put down his fork and reached for his wallet. He pulled out a piece of folded paper. "Would you like me to contact one of them, or do you want to take care of it yourself?" he asked, passing the paper to Mark and asking him to give it to Grampa.

Grampa Will accepted the list of names with a loud *"Grumpff!"* and tucked it into the pocket of his worn-out sweater. Nothing else was mentioned that evening about ghostwriters, books, or the list of names.

Despite the improving weather, the weekend was a gloomy one—especially for Mark. Sibyl kept reminding him how dumb it had been to advertise for a ghostwriter in the first place. "I thought you suggested the idea," he retorted.

But Sibyl insisted that *agreeing* that Grampa needed a ghostwriter and then advertising for one were two different things *entirely.*

After school on Monday, Sibyl was supposed to go to Jenny White's house to work on their book reports together. She stopped at home first to pick up her reading notebook and to tell her mother where she would be. But the girl never made it to Jenny's house that afternoon as planned! Considering what happened, it was quite understandable!

"Hi, little toot!" Sibyl greeted her younger brother as she walked through the muddy yard.

Jeremy stood on the front porch wearing a bright red stocking cap and red mittens. Instead of running to greet her as he usually did, the little boy simply walked toward his sister. His shoulders drooped with sadness. He took one of Sibyl's hands with his two mittened ones and gave it a tug. "Grampa has a lady in his house," he said, his large blue eyes filled with worry.

"Who is she?" Sibyl wanted to know. Jeremy shrugged. "Well, what kind of lady is she then?" Sibyl asked. Perhaps it was one of the women from the church paying Grampa Will a visit, she thought.

"A shiny-water lady," Jeremy answered.

"A what?" his sister exclaimed. "What do you mean?"

"She's like shiny water," the little boy tried to explain. "Like tinsel on our Christmas tree."

Sibyl didn't understand. Maybe Jeremy was describing the mysterious woman's clothing. "C'mon," she said, taking the small boy by the shoulder. "I want to meet this lady myself and say hello to Grampa before I go to Jenny's."

"But Grampa told me to go home," Jeremy protested. "And he said it *mean!*"

Sibyl was speechless. She couldn't imagine Grampa Will speaking harshly to Jeremy. The man doted on the little boy—almost as much as she did. He had never raised his voice to Jeremy before.

"Well, there must be a good reason," Sibyl said doubtfully. She took her brother into the house and helped him to remove his coat. Then she settled him in the family room with a glass of milk and a brownie.

"You work on these," she said, presenting him with a stack of wooden puzzles. "When I get back I'll tell you all about Grampa's visitor."

Mrs. Gaffney was seated at the dining room table, the one the family used only when they had company or for special occasions. She had books and papers spread out before her, and she looked very absorbed in her genealogy research. Mrs. Gaffney had gone back to college to get her master's degree in history and had homework every day, just like her two older children.

Sibyl started to ask her mom about Grampa's lady visitor and then changed her mind. She would soon find out for herself who the lady was and what she was doing at Grampa Will's.

"Hi! Bye!" Sibyl greeted her mother. "Jeremy's in the family room, and I'm going to Grampa's for a minute. Then I'm going to Jenny's house to work on our book reports. May I take Grampa a brownie?"

Mrs. Gaffney nodded, looking up just long enough to smile at her daughter and then resumed her work.

With two brownies in a paper napkin, Sibyl raced to the coach house. Her curiosity had reached its highest peak. Tapping briskly on the door and hollering "Ahoy!" Sibyl let herself in. What she saw erased any thoughts of Jenny and book reports from her mind.

There sat Grampa Will in his favorite chair, wearing his old gray sweater with the patches at the elbows. He was talking politely to Jeremy's shiny-water lady.

The woman, *if* you could call her that, did glimmer like sunlight on a lake. But it was quite obvious that she was not a *real* woman—not a flesh-and-blood woman! Sibyl gasped loudly. Actually, she gave more of a startled squeal. If Sibyl had been the screaming sort, she would have let out a bloodcurdling shriek, because her grandfather sat conversing with what *had* to be—could *only* be—a ghost!

"Sibyl, come in and shut the door," Grampa Will said gruffly. It was a command and not an invitation. But Sibyl could not move. She stood paralyzed by disbelief and fright.

"I thought . . . you . . . might like . . . er . . . some brownies," she stammered.

"Forget the brownies! Come here!" Grampa demanded.

Sibyl found that she couldn't make her legs move. She simply stood where she was, her mouth gaping, her eyes fixed on the ghostly female who sat so rigidly erect on Grampa's sofa. She was dressed like a fashionable lady from another era. Her dress was a dark blue, multitiered one with stiff petticoats underneath. There were lacy ruffles at her throat and wrists. A quaint-looking shawl was draped around her shoulders. From the tips of her high-buttoned shoes to the top of her snow-white head with its ringlets, the lady spook was a perfect picture of ghostly gentility.

"I think . . . I think I'm going to . . . to throw up!" Sibyl declared. Placing her free hand over her mouth, she darted out of the room.

"How extraordinarily rude!" Sibyl heard the ghostly figure exclaim in a shocked voice—a voice that was surprisingly clear and normal for a spook!

Three

THE POSITION IS FILLED

"I *was* somewhat hesitant about applying for this position," the ghostly woman was saying to Grampa Will when Sibyl returned meekly to the living room, this time without her coat or the brownies. "For you see, I'm not really a *professional,* don't you know. I mean, no one has ever *paid* me to be a ghost, and I've certainly had no professional training," she admitted. She smoothed one of the many flounces of her long, full-skirted dress.

"One day I was severely ill with influenza and then, *poof!* the next thing I know, I'm a ghost! I must have died, don't you know. But I've never felt better! No more pains in my joints, and my knees don't snap and crackle like they used to."

Sibyl crept up slowly behind her grandfather's chair and placed a cold, trembling hand on his shoulder. He reached up to pat her hand reassuringly, but his eyes never left the smiling face of his phantom guest.

The ghost gave Sibyl a quick, disapproving glance and then addressed Grampa Will again.

"Your advertisement was so intriguing that I simply couldn't resist applying," she declared. "Even though I'm not a professional ghost, I've had one hundred and nine years of experience. There's so little for a ghost to do. I told myself it certainly wouldn't hurt to apply. I did want to try my hand at writing stories, and I am quite a good speller," she added proudly.

"How did you come to see the ad in the newspaper?" Grampa wanted to know.

"Oh, I frequently drift in and out of the public library and read a little and watch the people," the ghost answered.

"Are you an *exceptional* speller?" Grampa asked. Sibyl was surprised! How could Grampa sit there calmly conversing with this—this spook as though it—*she*—was just an Avon lady? And surely, Sibyl thought with a stab of panic, *surely* he was not thinking of hiring her!

"I *am* an exceptional speller!" the ghost said confidently, and proceeded to prove it. "Lexicography. L-e-x-i-c-o-g-r-a-p-h-y." Finished, she beamed at Grampa Will. "Compendium," she began. "C-o-m," but Grampa interrupted her.

"Fine, fine! That's fine!" he insisted. "I can see that you are a very good speller. What you can't spell, you could no doubt look up in the dictionary."

"Naturally!" she replied primly with a quick nod of her head that made her white sausagelike ringlets dance.

"But my grandfather doesn't want a *ghost*

ghost!" Sibyl declared, unable to keep silent any longer. "He advertised for a ghost*writer!*"

"Just who are *you,* young lady?" the ghost queried.

"The question is who are *you?*" Sibyl replied in an awed whisper.

"*I* am Tallulah Farquar," the apparition answered.

"*I* am Sibyl Gaffney, and this is my grandfather," she said, amazed that she was conversing with a real ghost.

"How do you do?" Tallulah said pertly. Sibyl just nodded, thankful that the ghost had not offered to shake hands.

"Do you type?" Grampa Will asked.

"What is 'type'?" Tallulah asked.

"Writing with a typewriter," Sibyl explained. When Tallulah still looked confused, Sibyl added, "A typewriter is sort of a writing machine."

"Similar to a printing press?" Tallulah asked, tilting her head to one side. Sibyl and Grandpa exchanged exasperated looks. Before either one of them could attempt a further explanation, there was a thundering knock at the door, followed by a boisterous "Ahoy!"

Mark came bounding in. His mouth dropped open at the sight of Tallulah Farquar sitting primly on the sofa. He let out a hoarse croak.

"Oh, I do hope *he's* not going to be sick too," Tallulah said with feeling. "It's so rude, don't you know."

"I don't b-believe it!" Mark stammered. "It looks like—she must be . . . a ghost!" He approached his grandfather's chair with considerable caution, his eyes never leaving the strange, shimmering vision on the sofa. "Grampa, where did you find—it—her?" he asked breathlessly.

"He didn't find *me,* young man!" Tallulah declared loftily. "*I* found him."

"This is my older brother," Sibyl put in, addressing her grandfather's unusual guest. "And this is Miss Tallulah Farquar . . . er . . . at least she *was* Miss Farquar . . . once."

"She's come to inquire about that ad of yours," Grampa Will said with an unmistakable twinkle in his eyes.

Mark stared at his sister, who stood smiling at him, enjoying her brother's disbelief. He didn't know what surprised him more—the fact that there was a ghost sitting on Grampa's sofa or that Grampa Will was actually talking to her so calmly. It was as if Grampa were accustomed to conversing with phantoms daily.

"Is he the one wanting a ghost?" Tallulah asked, indicating Mark with a shimmering finger that peeped out of a dainty crocheted half glove.

"No! We didn't want a *ghost* at all!" Mark blurted out. Then seeing the obvious disappointment on Tallulah's face, he put in quickly, "It's a ghost*writer* we want. Someone who will help my grandfather write his autobiography. A professional."

"So Simplicity has been telling me," Tallulah replied crisply.

"My name is Sibyl," she reminded the ghost. But Tallulah did not appear to notice.

"The advertisement clearly read 'professional ghost wanted.' It said nothing at all about a professional writer," Tallulah pointed out.

"Well, yes, I know what it said—" Mark began.

"I *am* a ghost!" Tallulah interrupted him. "And I *do* know how to write. I would welcome the opportunity to help Mr. Gnatly write his book."

"Gaffney." Grampa corrected her with an amused grin.

"And she *is* an exceptional speller," Sibyl said with a smirk.

"Yes, indeed I am!" Tallulah affirmed. "Why, I can spell just about anything! I won all the spelling bees when I was in grammar school. Epithlium. E-p-i-t-h-l-i-u-m."

"I don't believe it!" Mark declared. "A ghost that spells! *There are no such things as ghosts*!" He looked directly at Sibyl. Surely, she didn't believe in ghosts, even if there was one right before their eyes. But Sibyl met his gaze with a smile and simply shrugged.

"Mr. Grundy," Tallulah said very seriously, "I want this position. I know I am not exactly what you had in mind . . ."

"You can say *that* again!" Sibyl murmured.

"But if you will accept my services temporarily, you will not be disappointed. And what's more," Miss Farquar said, sitting up quite straight and dignified, "I won't charge a single cent."

"You would do it for free?" Mark asked unbelievingly.

"Certainly!" Tallulah replied. "What do I need with money? I do not require food or clothing, and I do not pay for my lodgings. You see, I simply have no need for money. What I *do* need, however, is employment. Something to occupy my time. I am *so* bored!"

"By the way, where do you live?" Sibyl asked, coming around the corner of Grampa's chair. In spite of her dismay and disbelief, she found herself warming toward the quaint ghost.

"Not far from here," Tallulah responded. "I live in a big old house around the corner. It has been empty for quite some time. I've lived in this part of town all my life," she added. "I can remember when it was called Postville. It wasn't until eighteen-fifty-three that the town was named Lincoln—after a young Illinois lawyer."

"Abraham Lincoln!" Mark exclaimed. "We learned about all this in school. It's the only town ever named after Lincoln *before* he became president."

"That's right." Tallulah nodded, her white ringlets bobbing about like springs. "And he christened the town with the juice of a watermelon. I was there at the depot that day waiting for my Aunt Rachel to arrive on the train from Springfield. I saw the whole thing!" She beamed at them proudly. Mark and Sibyl began to think that having a ghost around could be very educational.

"Would you be able to work each weekday and occasionally on Saturdays?" Grampa asked abruptly. The children were stunned.

"Grampa, you can't be serious!" Mark exclaimed, bolting upright.

"Grumpff!" was Grampa's only response.

"Why not?" Sibyl wanted to know after considerable silence. "She might turn out to be a great writer. We already know how well she can spell."

"But she's a—a—ghost!" Mark reminded his sister. "I mean, she's just a figment of our imaginations, isn't she? Maybe we are all a bit feverish or something. *You* don't believe in ghosts, do you, Grampa?"

"Feverish?" Tallulah asked with a note of concern in her voice. "I was quite feverish with the influenza and then *poof!* I became a ghost."

"What are we going to tell Mom and Dad?" Mark asked. "That Grampa hired a real ghost instead of a ghostwriter to help him with his book?"

"Grumpff!" Grampa replied, studying Tallulah from under his heavy white eyebrows.

"We don't *have* to tell them, do we, Grampa?" Sibyl asked, looking down on her grandfather's pink and shiny bald spot. But before the elderly man could answer, Mark coughed loudly. He rolled his eyes in the direction of the sofa. Tallulah, who had been very visible before, was fading from view. Sibyl blinked once or twice and could have sworn that the shimmering apparition wasn't there at all!

"Miss Farquar, are you still with us?" Grampa asked, leaning forward in his chair. "Miss Farquar?"

The female phantom once again glittered discernibly. She was wringing her hands and seemed considerably distressed. "I do beg your pardon, Mr. Gwaltney," she apologized. "Was I fading away?"

"The name's Gaffney! Will Gaffney! And, yes, you almost disappeared altogether."

"I am so sorry," Tallulah apologized. "But making oneself visible takes a bit of effort, don't you know. And if one does not concentrate, one simply fades from view."

"You mean you're only visible when you want to be?" Mark asked.

"But of course!" Tallulah said as if the boy should have known this already. She rose to her feet. Grampa Will stood also. "If you would be so good as to tell me whether or not you have accepted me for the position," Tallulah said in a polite but weary voice. "I am a bit worn out, don't you know."

"Miss Farquar . . . the position is yours," Grampa Will said after a moment's hesitation. "I will supply the pens and paper, and you may write my story in longhand. I'll have someone else do the typing."

"Grampa! You don't mean it!" Mark and Sibyl declared in unison.

"Thank you, Mr. Daphne," Tallulah murmured gratefully. She chose to ignore the horror-stricken faces of the two youngsters. "I'll be here tomorrow at nine, if that's all right with you."

"Yes, that will be fine," Grampa said, paying no attention to Sibyl's frantic tugging on his sleeve. "And the name is Gaffney. Let me see you to the door."

"There's no need," Tallulah said, glimmering gaily. "Until tomorrow then," and with that, she fluttered through the room like a gentle breeze and drifted through the wall.

Grampa Will stood staring after her, while Mark collapsed weakly into the chair his grandfather had vacated. Sibyl sat down on the sofa and put her hand on the spot where Tallulah had been sitting.

"It isn't even warm," she said to no one in particular. "She sat here all that time, and it isn't even a little bit warm."

"Why did you do it, Grampa?" Mark demanded. "How could you hire a ghost? *You* don't believe in ghosts, do you? There *are* no such things as ghosts and goblins *anyway!*"

Grampa sighed. "Mark, when I was a boy there were no supersonic jets—I went to Africa on a ship. Man only dreamed of going to the moon and we couldn't even imagine such things as heart transplants. Microwave ovens, high-tech computers, and even televisions weren't even dreamed of," he said. "So, you see, an old-fashioned ghost isn't such a hard thing for me to believe in at all."

After a moment of reflective silence, Mark and Sibyl glanced at each other questioningly. "What should we tell Mom and Dad?" she asked.

"You don't need to tell them anything," Grampa said gruffly.

"But what about the college student you are supposed to call to help you with your book?" Mark reminded him. "How are you going to tell Dad that you won't be needing a student helper after all?"

"I need someone to do the typing, don't I?" Grampa replied. "I'll have your father make the necessary arrangements. We won't mention Miss Farquar at all." Mark and Sibyl exchanged skeptical glances.

"And what about Jeremy?" Sibyl asked. "He saw the shiny-water lady—that's what he called her."

"He did?" Mark exclaimed. Sibyl nodded gloomily.

"I'll take care of Jeremy," their grandfather said, unperturbed. "I'll take care of everything." He slowly made his way to the coat closet and pulled his jacket from the hanger. "I'm going to walk down to the drugstore," he told them. "I need to get some of those yellow writing tablets and a package of pens."

Sibyl put on her coat too, and followed her grandfather and her brother out the door. She stood watching as the old man shuffled down the sidewalk toward the business district in town. "Well," she said turning to Mark, "there's one thing I can say for Tallulah Farquar. She's *very* interesting."

Still a bit dazed with disbelief, Mark only nodded. Tallulah Farquar was more than interesting. She was absolutely, positively fascinating!

Four

DOUBTFUL THOUGHTS

Mrs. Gaffney was taking Jeremy to the mall in Springfield and wanted to know if Sibyl would like to go along. There was no school today because of a teachers' conference. Sibyl loved the mall, and her mother was surprised when Sibyl said she didn't want to go.

"Are you feeling all right?" Mrs. Gaffney asked suspiciously.

"I'm just real tired," Sibyl answered truthfully. She had not slept well at all the night before. She had had dreams of haunted houses, ghosts, and a floating dictionary with words drifting out of its open pages. It wasn't easy to pass up a chance to go to White Oaks Mall, but if she stayed home, she would be able to see Tallulah again.

Mrs. Gaffney came over to the bed and pressed her hand against Sibyl's forehead. "Well, you don't have a temperature," she announced. "Perhaps you should stay home and just rest. You might be coming down with something. Drink lots of juice while I'm gone and dress warmly." She tucked the blankets more snugly under Sibyl's chin and then closed the door behind her as she quietly left the room.

Now that she was awake, Sibyl couldn't go back to sleep. She remained beneath the covers until she heard her mother and Jeremy leave the house. Sibyl then sprang out of bed. She dressed warmly in jeans and a bulky red pullover sweater and went downstairs for some toast and peanut butter.

"Hey, sibling!" Mark greeted her as she came into the kitchen. He stood by the counter slicing a banana into his cereal. "Are you really sick?"

"No!" Sibyl snapped. She was never in a good mood before breakfast, and she found Mark especially annoying on an empty stomach.

"But you didn't go to the mall with Mom," her brother declared. "You must be sicker than you think."

"You *know* why I didn't go!" Sibyl hissed at him. She put two slices of bread into the toaster. "And don't think of running over to Grampa's without me," she said, pointing the butter knife at him.

"I won't," Mark promised. "I want you to be with me when I see that ghost again. It makes me feel better to know that you can see her too. If you hadn't been there yesterday, I would have thought I was dreaming."

"You weren't dreaming," Sibyl assured him. "We both couldn't dream the same thing at the same time *and* with our eyes wide open." She brought her toast to the table and sat down across from Mark.

"It's past nine," Mark said, noting the time on the apple-shaped clock over the stove. "Do you think *she's* over there now?" Sibyl started to answer when Mr. Gaffney came into the kitchen from the basement. He carried several musty-smelling books.

"Good morning!" he said cheerfully, dropping the books onto the corner of the table. "I came to fortify my insides with some strong, hot coffee. It's cold down there!"

"What were you doing?" Mark asked, wondering why his father hadn't yet left for the college.

"The literature club is having a used book sale next week, and I thought this would be as good a time as any to sort through those boxes down there." He nodded his head in the direction of the door that led downstairs to the basement. "Besides, I only teach afternoon classes today. What are you two doing this morning?"

Sibyl and Mark exchanged cautious glances. They both knew that if they were not careful, one or even both of them would be drafted into helping their father with his book sorting.

"I promised Jenny White that I'd come over so we could work on our book reports together," Sibyl spoke up quickly. "I was going to go yesterday, but . . . er . . . something came up. I also promised Grampa that I would clean his microwave oven."

It had been over two weeks since she had offered to clean her grandfather's microwave. She'd be glad to do it for a dollar, Sibyl had told him, but until this moment she had completely forgotten. Mark's eyes widened as though he thought his sister were telling a lie.

"I've got a paper to do," he admitted, glaring at Sibyl. "I have to write an essay about someone I admire. I thought I'd use Grampa Will as my subject. I'm going over to talk to him about it as soon as I've finished my breakfast."

"Well, then," their father said, spooning sugar into his coffee, "would one of you take these books over when you go? They're his, but I'm sure Grampa's forgotten all about them. H. Rider Haggard novels. Have you ever read one?" he asked with an inquiring smile. When both youngsters shook their heads, he declared, "You'd enjoy them, I think. They are like Indiana Jones adventures."

Sibyl excused herself from the table and raced upstairs to change from her slippers into knee socks and ankle boots. She ran a brush quickly through her short tangle of brown curls. She watched with dismay as the static electricity made her hair stand out like a dandelion gone to seed. Smoothing her hair down the best she could, Sibyl stuck her tongue out at herself and then returned to the kitchen.

Mark was already on the back porch with his coat and the old books tucked under his arm. Mr. Gaffney was nowhere in sight, and Sibyl assumed that he had returned to his book sorting in the basement. "I thought I'd better wait for you," Mark said with a sheepish grin.

"Chicken!" Sibyl exclaimed. "You're just afraid of ghosts!"

Together, they made their way to their grandfather's and knocked briskly on the door. When they had "ahoyed," they let themselves in. Grampa was pacing slowly back and forth across the living room floor, dictating hesitantly to his ghostly assistant. She was really there! As plain as day—or as plain as a ghost can be. She sat at the desk writing Grampa's words down onto a yellow tablet.

"Good morning, Grampa," Mark and Sibyl greeted him in unison as they hung up their coats. Mark set the old books down on the telephone table.

"Oh, dear me, you cannot stay!" Tallulah Farquar exclaimed, rising quickly from the desk and fluttering toward them. Her full skirt billowed out around her feet. Her white curls, like neat little sausages, bounced around her face. "Your grandfather has been inspired. He must write while the Muse is with him."

"The what?" Mark asked.

"You two run along," Grampa Will said. "Miss Farquar and I have lots of work to do this morning."

"But I'm here to clean your microwave oven," Sibyl protested.

"Come back this afternoon, children, and we'll

have a little tea," Miss Farquar chirped, waving the youngsters toward the door.

"Yes, come back later," Grampa agreed. Opening the door for Mark and Sibyl, he repeated, "We have lots of work to do. You understand. I'll see you later on."

Mark and Sibyl found themselves out in the cold, standing on the front step, the door shut firmly in their faces. "Can you believe that?" Mark exclaimed, staring at his sister in disbelief.

"We've been kicked out!" she replied. "And I don't like it!"

"Neither do I!" Mark huffed. Thrusting his hands down into his coat pockets, he turned back to the Big House. "Inspired!" he declared with a snort.

"It's weird," Sibyl said, walking along slowly beside her brother."We're actually leaving Grampa Will in there with a ghost."

"Yeah, and a bossy one at that," Mark added.

"Ghosts don't take over your mind or your body or anything like that, do they?" Sibyl asked.

"How should I know?" her brother snapped. "I don't really know anything about ghosts."

"Well, one of us should find out something about them," Sibyl said. "She could be dangerous. She might brainwash Grampa or drink his blood."

"Ghosts don't drink blood," Mark said, rolling his eyes.

"How do you know?" Sibyl retorted. "You just

said you didn't know anything about ghosts!" Before Mark could protest, his sister added, "Go to the library and get some books about spooks."

"Why me?" Mark wanted to know, pausing at the back door.

"Because it was your brainy idea to advertise for a ghost in the first place," Sibyl reminded him. "And now we've got one."

"She isn't what I was expecting, you know," Mark said, lowering his voice as they entered the house.

"But she's what we got!" Sibyl whispered back. After a moment's pause, she added, "I think Grampa likes her."

Her brother merely answered with a loud, *"Grumpff!"*

For Sibyl, the rest of the morning seemed to crawl along like one of the fuzzy woolly worms that inch their way slowly across the Illinois roads and sidewalks in the fall. Mark, after going down into the basement to tell his father where he was going, made off for the public library which was only four blocks away.

Sibyl curled up on her bed with a mystery. She couldn't seem to concentrate on the words though. Her thoughts were torn between worrying about Grampa Will and regretting that she hadn't gone to the mall with her mom. She soon fell asleep and didn't wake up until her father tapped on her bedroom door.

"Do you want a bowl of chili?" he asked, poking his head around the door.

"Is it lunchtime already?" Sibyl asked. "Is Mark back yet?"

"Yes, it's time for lunch, and no, your brother is not back," Mr. Gaffney replied.

"Dad, do you know anything about ghosts?" Sibyl asked, crawling off the bed and following her father downstairs.

"They haunt houses," was her dad's unexpected response. Sibyl had been sure that he would say that there were no such things as ghosts.

"I mean, do they have special powers or anything like that?" she asked. "According to the legends and stories about them," she added hastily.

"I couldn't tell you, honey," Mr. Gaffney confessed, filling a bowl with steaming chili for her. "As far as I know, they just glide up and down staircases, groaning and rattling their chains. Why do you ask?"

"No reason," Sibyl lied.

"There are some people who take ghosts and haunted houses very seriously," her father went on. "But I'm not one of them." He broke a handful of crackers into his chili bowl. Sibyl watched him but didn't say anything. She couldn't help wondering what her dad would say if he knew that at this very moment Grampa Will was dictating chapter one of his autobiography to a ghost.

Sibyl longed to blurt out the truth—to tell him

that ghosts *were* real. But she didn't. Grampa had said that he would take care of everything. Sibyl would have to trust him to do so.

As she poured herself a glass of milk, Mr. Gaffney got up from the table and carried his empty bowl to the sink. "I'm going over to see Grampa for a minute," he told her. "I'll be right back."

Sibyl jumped from her seat, spilling her milk all over the table. "Don't bother Grampa now!" she called out. But it was too late! Her father had darted out the back door, without a coat, and was walking briskly toward the coach house.

Sibyl rushed to the back door and stood there in her stockinged feet, her arms crossed over her chest. She watched her father approach Grampa's door. He knocked twice and then let himself in. "Oh, Mark!" she moaned quietly. "Where *are* you?"

Five

TALLULAH IN CHARGE

Shivering from the cold and sudden anxiety, Sibyl went back into the kitchen to wipe up the spilt milk. She wondered what was going on at this very minute in her grandfather's living room. And why wasn't Mark back from the library yet? She had just refilled her milk glass when she heard her father open the back door. He paused briefly to stamp the slush off his shoes.

"What's Grampa doing?" Sibyl asked eagerly. She searched her father's face for any signs of shock or confusion. But he was only grinning.

"Dad's working on that book of his." Mr. Gaffney chuckled. "He's got several pages done already. He's really taking the whole thing seriously."

Sibyl was dying to ask, Was he alone? but she didn't dare. Instead, she asked, "Do you think it's a good thing for Grampa to spend so much time by himself?"

"By himself?" Her father laughed. Sibyl felt her heart beat a frantic *thud-thud*. "He just told me that you kids never give him a moment's peace. He said that one or both of you is always over there."

"Grampa said *that?*" Sibyl asked. She tried not to look as hurt as she felt. After all, she thought, they only went over there so Grampa Will wouldn't be lonely.

"Yes, he certainly did," her father replied. "I don't want you kids to bother him so often. He seems quite intent on producing his book, and we should give him all the encouragement and cooperation that he needs. And if that means leaving him alone so he can get some writing done, then I expect you kids to leave him alone."

"But he's not—" Sibyl began, and then bit her lip. She had almost admitted that Grampa Will was *not* alone over there at all! He had a ghost in his living room! A wily, bossy, female phantom who had practically thrown Grampa's own grandchildren out of his house!

"But he's not what?" her father asked.

"Never mind," Sibyl replied. She was beginning to feel more and more frantic about Grampa's new arrangements. And where was Mark? Why wasn't he here to help her worry?

"Well, I've got to make a quick trip to the hardware store, and then I'm going to the college," Mr. Gaffney announced. "Tell your mother not to bother making dinner. I'll bring home a couple of pizzas."

After her father had gone, Sibyl loaded all the dirty dishes into the dishwasher and retreated to the family room. She curled up on the sofa, wrapped like a cocoon in a blue and brown afghan to wait for Mark. He returned home an hour later.

"Where have you been?" she demanded, rushing into the kitchen to meet him, the afghan draped around her like a cape. "What took you so long?"

"I ran into Jeff Browning," Mark said simply, as though that should explain everything.

"Great! Just great!" Sibyl exclaimed. "While you're out running all over town with the dumbest sixth grader in the whole school, I was stuck here to worry all by myself! I had to handle all of the emergencies alone!"

"What emergencies?" Mark was eager to know. He placed a book on the counter and peeked curiously into the chili pot on the back of the stove.

"Dad went over to Grampa's!" Sibyl told him. "What happened to all those books you were going to bring back?"

"I thought Dad might get suspicious if I came home with a stack of books on spooks," Mark explained. "So I sort of skimmed through them at the library and brought the best one home."

"It looks hard to read, and there aren't any pictures," Sibyl observed as she flipped through the pages. As soon as she'd said that, Sibyl was sorry. Mark was always rubbing it in that she wasn't as good a student as he was. She waited for the usual attack on her low grades.

But Mark was more interested in their father's visit to the coach house. "What happened?" he asked.

"Nothing that I know of," Sibyl admitted. "But Grampa told Dad that we were over there all the time and that he can't get any work done."

"Grampa said *that?*" Mark asked, looking as surprised as his sister had been. "I bet *she* put him up to it. I don't think it's such a good idea to leave Grampa Will over there alone with *her.*"

"I don't trust her!" Sibyl said hotly. "I don't trust her one little bit!"

"I'm going over there right now!" Mark said, pounding his fist on the counter. "Are you coming with me or not?"

"Just let me get my shoes," Sibyl replied. She darted into the family room to retrieve her sneakers. She'd been dying to go back over to Grampa's all day. Who did that Tallulah Farquar think she was anyway? Telling them to come back for tea! Well, now was just as good a time for tea as any other, Sibyl decided.

"This time we'll leave when we are darn good and ready!" she told her brother as they marched to the coach house.

"You said it!" Mark exclaimed. Sibyl thought he looked as though he were ready for a fight. Mark looked even more threatening when they discovered that Grampa's front door was locked! He pounded on the door fiercely. Sibyl watched her older brother smolder with anger. She felt angry too.

"Come in, come in!" Grampa Will greeted them warmly, opening the door for them. "No need to break the door down, you know," he said with a smile. "We were just getting ready to have a little snack," he told the kids as they removed their coats. He never once explained the locked door.

Mark and Sibyl exchanged looks of dismay at the word *we*. Following their grandfather into the small kitchen, they saw Tallulah putting small, triangle-shaped ham salad sandwiches on a plate.

"Good afternoon, Matthew, Semele!" she said gaily. "Have a seat, won't you, and have a cookie." She passed them a plate of gingersnaps. Sibyl noted that Tallulah moved about the kitchen as though she was quite at home here.

"How about some hot chocolate?" Grampa Will asked them, pulling two mugs from the cabinet.

"Oh, let me do it, Wilbur!" the ghost offered, flitting over to the counter with a box of instant hot chocolate mix in one of her shimmering hands.

"Wilbur!" Sibyl exclaimed. It was bad enough that Miss Farquar couldn't get *their* names straight—Matthew and Semele, indeed! But Grampa's name was certainly *not* Wilbur! "Grampa's name is William," she said with a frown. Sibyl was surprised to see that Grampa was smiling happily as though it didn't matter at all that Tallulah had called him by the wrong name—again!

Mark was surprised too, but for a different reason. He wondered when Grampa and the ghost had gotten on a first-name basis. He watched as Tallulah filled the mugs with water and then placed them in the microwave oven. After a minute or so of intense concentration, she touched the appropriate buttons to heat the water. Tallulah smiled at Grampa Will who beamed right back at her.

"Tallulah fell in love with this newfangled oven of mine," he confided to Mark and Sibyl. "I've been showing her the wonders of the twentieth century: ballpoint pens, flush toilets, the refrigerator, the television."

"All so marvelous!" Tallulah exclaimed, removing the mugs from the microwave and stirring in the cocoa mix. "Especially this food that cooks itself."

"Did you get much writing done?" Mark asked somewhat sternly. He reached for another gingersnap.

"Yes, we did. Fourteen pages!" Grampa Will looked quite pleased. "This is working out much better than I had hoped." Mark threw Sibyl a highly skeptical glance.

"Quite so!" Tallulah agreed, bringing the hot chocolate to the table with a smile.

"Aren't you tired of being visible yet?" Sibyl asked unexpectedly. "Don't you need to go home and rest?" She had noticed that Tallulah was far from being dim and faded. She wondered how that was possible since Tallulah had been with Grampa Will since early that morning.

Her grandfather chuckled. He apparently found the question an amusing one. Tallulah sat down at the table and pushed the sandwiches and cookies in Grampa's direction. "I'm not tired, dear," she gurgled happily, addressing Sibyl. "Wilfred so thoughtfully suggested that—"

"William!" Sibyl corrected her.

"Yes, William, certainly," the interrupted ghost agreed. "He suggested that I relax and not worry about being visible, don't you know."

"It was the craziest thing I ever saw!" Grampa laughed. "That pen was just moving back and forth across the paper all by itself!" He laughed so hard that he began to choke. It struck Mark and Sibyl that they had not seen their grandfather enjoy himself so much since Nana Rosa had died.

"And when Thaddeus . . . er . . . your father . . . stopped by, I simply put down the pen and sat very, very still." Tallulah tittered. "He never even guessed that I was there." Then with a happy sigh, the ghost added, "I can't remember when I've had a more entertaining morning. And such an interesting one, too. It's so fascinating listening to your grandfather's stories about his journey to Africa. He helped build a medical clinic deep in the Liberian jungle—did you know?"

"Yes, we do know," Mark said dryly.

"Tallulah has two brothers," Grampa Will then informed them. "One went off to California in eighteen-fifty to look for gold."

"That was Ezekiel," Tallulah told the children. "We called him Zeke. He was quite an adventurer."

"And her younger brother joined the Union army and fought in the War Between the States," Grampa added.

"*His* name was Jeremiah," Tallulah put in. "He was killed in the war. It nearly broke my poor mother's heart. Jerry was her baby." Her small round face looked suddenly wistful.

Sibyl glanced at her brother. She could see that he was intrigued. Mark loved history and was especially interested in the Civil War period. While Sibyl did not doubt that Tallulah had had two brothers, she wouldn't have bet any money on the ghost's chances of remembering their names correctly.

"In those days, my hair was brown. Just like yours, Sarah," Tallulah said.

"Sibyl," the girl corrected her. She tried to imagine those shimmering curls in any other color, but she couldn't. "Did you have children?" Sibyl asked.

"I never married," Tallulah replied. Sibyl could have sworn that the ghost blushed.

"We need to get back to work now, Tallulah," Grampa said courteously. He scooted his chair back away from the table and reached for the empty mugs and plates. Tallulah whisked them away before he could do so and carried them to the kitchen sink.

As Mark and Sibyl said their reluctant good-byes and put on their coats, Grampa Will amazed his phantom friend with hot and cold running water coming out of a single spigot.

"Isn't that something about her brothers?" Mark exclaimed a little while later when he and Sibyl were outside. "Do you think they are ghosts, too?"

"Did you see the way she made herself right at home in Grampa's kitchen?" Sibyl asked, ignoring Mark's question.

"You know what? I almost wish I could do my essay on Tallulah!" Mark declared.

"She's bossy!" Sibyl reminded him with a disapproving glare.

"Yes, she is," Mark acknowledged. "Sort of. Maybe that's why nobody ever married her."

"I think she's trying to take charge," Sibyl said gloomily. She and Mark stepped in through the back door of the Big House. They removed their coats and shoes in silence. Both were thinking about all they had heard and seen over at Grampa Will's and trying to make sense of it all.

"I think she's a hard worker," Mark declared. "She and Grampa get along so well too."

"He *does* seem to like her," Sibyl agreed. "He seems to like her a lot, even though she never gets his name right!"

Six

GRAMPA TAKES CARE OF EVERYTHING

Grampa had promised to take care of Jeremy's curiosity. One fine, springlike morning in early March, he did just that. The little boy had been playing outside with his wagon and his fleet of toy trucks. Mrs. Gaffney had ordered him not to bother Grampa Will, who was busy writing a book. But Jeremy missed his grandfather's company. He marched out back to the Little House and pounded on the door with his small fist.

It was a beautiful day—too beautiful to spend by himself. His daddy was at work and his brother and sister were at school. Mommy was busy. Jeremy knew that if he could get Grampa to come outside for just a minute he might be persuaded to go for a walk. After all, Jeremy reasoned, there were plenty of books in the world already. He'd seen them all at the library. It would be a sad thing to waste a sunny morning writing another one.

Jeremy knocked at the door again. He then pulled and tugged at the door handle until Grampa opened the door from the inside. "Good morning, Jeremy!"

Jeremy smiled up at Grampa Will and entered the house without being invited in. Hoodwink, the big orange cat, followed him in. He slipped in quickly between the small boy's legs, and Jeremy almost stumbled. Suddenly, the cat arched its back and snarled angrily at something shimmering there at the desk. Jeremy thought he saw something too, but when he looked again, it was gone.

"Do you want to write a book or go for a walk?" the little boy asked. He turned up his hopeful face to look into his grandfather's smiling one.

"It is a mighty fine morning for a walk," Grampa Will acknowledged. His face softened as he looked down at his youngest grandson. "I think I could tear myself away from my work for a while."

"Maybe we could go to the park and you could push me on a swing," Jeremy suggested.

"Why not!" Grampa Will replied. "But first I must tell my make-believe friend that I'm going out for the morning. Tallulah!" he called.

The ghost reappeared in the chair at the desk where she'd been sitting quietly and invisibly. Hoodwink fled under the couch with a terrified screech. Jeremy stared and stared. He slipped his small hand into Grampa Will's large one and held on tight.

"Tallulah, I'm going to take the rest of the morning off," Grampa told her. "Jeremy has pointed out, and rightly so, that it is a fine day for a walk."

"Indeed, it is!" Tallulah agreed with a smile.

"She's the shiny-water lady," Jeremy said, pointing a hesitant finger at his grandfather's spooky friend.

"That's Tallulah. She's my make-believe friend," Grampa informed him. "She isn't real, you know."

"But I can see her," Jeremy insisted.

"That's because you have an active imagination," Grampa Will said. He placed his large, rough hand on top of Jeremy's blond head.

"Is that a good thing to have?" Jeremy asked.

"Oh, yes, indeed!" his grandfather exclaimed. "You can't have too much imagination, I always say. Now, you run into the kitchen and get some of those cookies on the table in there. We'll want something to munch on while we take our walk."

As Jeremy scampered off to get the cookies, Grampa Will made arrangements for Tallulah to come back that afternoon. She gladly agreed to do so. She even offered to stay late and prepare dinner for Grampa Will. Although Tallulah did not eat, she enjoyed puttering around in Grampa's kitchen. She often prepared meals that had, at first, made Grampa raise his bushy eyebrows dubiously. But he had enjoyed rinktum ditty and English monkey—both egg and cheese dishes. Now he didn't mind giving Tallulah free run in the kitchen.

"Do you have eggs? A bit of cooked beef? Some cheese?" Tallulah asked. Grampa replied that he did. "Good! I'll scramble up some frizzle dizzle for your supper," she declared and then glided effortlessly through the window. She disappeared just as Jeremy was returning with his fists full of gingersnaps.

Grampa Will retrieved his jacket from the closet and accepted a handful of cookies from Jeremy. He then coaxed Hoodwink out from under the sofa and shooed the cat out the door. Together Grampa and Jeremy went to the Big House to tell Mrs. Gaffney that they were planning a leisurely walk and an early lunch at the coffee shop downtown.

"Jeremy! I thought I told you not to bother your grandfather!" Mrs. Gaffney scolded. She momentarily put aside the clean clothes she had been folding.

"He didn't bother me at all," Grampa said, still holding Jeremy's hand. "In fact, I was looking for an excuse to get out of the house for a while. All work and no play makes Grampa a dull writer," he quipped.

"You boys have a good time, then," Mrs. Gaffney said after hearing their plans.

Grampa and Jeremy *did* have a good time. That evening around the dinner table, Jeremy told everybody about having hot dogs and fries for lunch and swinging in the park and seeing purple croakers in the grass.

"What's a purple croaker?" Mark asked, helping himself to more mashed potatoes.

"It's a little flower," Jeremy told him. There

was a tiny note of pride in his voice. He knew something his big brother didn't even know!

"I think he means a crocus," Mrs. Gaffney put in.

"That's what I said," Jeremy insisted. He held out his plate and asked for another piece of fried chicken. "Grampa Will's having frizzly dizzly for dinner tonight," he said unexpectedly.

"And what in the world is frizzly dizzly?" his father asked.

"I don't know," the little boy confessed. After taking a sip of his milk, he added, "Lulu is making it for him."

"And who is Lulu?" Mrs. Gaffney wanted to know.

"Grampa's make-believe friend," Jeremy replied innocently. Mark choked on his food then. He stared in horror at his sister whose eyes were nearly popping out of her head.

"So, Grampa has a make-believe friend named Lulu, does he?" Mr. Gaffney said, helping himself to more peas. He winked at his wife and smiled. Mrs. Gaffney smiled back.

"She wears long dresses and has funny curls," Jeremy added. "She's old, too, like a grandma."

"How do you know?" Sibyl asked. Her voice trembled. She and Mark had tried their best to keep their little brother away from the coach house when Tallulah Farquar was there. They had consistently ignored his questions about the shiny-water lady and hoped that if he didn't see her again, he would soon forget all about her.

"So, how do you know what she looks like?" Sibyl repeated nervously.

"I saw her," the boy said simply.

"But how can you see her if she's Grampa's make-believe friend?" Mrs. Gaffney asked, looking up from her plate.

"Grampa said it is because I have an activity machine," Jeremy answered. He took another swallow of milk, which left a white mustache on his upper lip.

"What's that—an activity machine?" Mark asked. He was too nervous now to eat any more.

Jeremy shrugged. After a moment's consideration, Mr. Gaffney asked, "Did Grampa say you have an active imagination?"

Jeremy's face lit up. "Yes! That's it! Grampa said I have one of those!"

"You can say that again!" Mark declared with exaggerated enthusiasm. He knew that he couldn't let his parents get any ideas about Jeremy's tales being truthful ones. Silently, he thanked Tallulah for offering to make one of her old-fashioned suppers for Grampa tonight. Frizzly dizzly, indeed! No one would believe that *that* was anything but a product of Jeremy's active imagination!

"Pass the biscuits, please," Sibyl said then. Handing the bread basket to his sister, Mark noted that she was smiling. In fact, Sibyl looked quite pleased about something. He thought he could guess what it was. Grampa Will had told them that he would take care of Jeremy's curiosity, and he had done just that!

Everything was working out just fine. Jeremy's curiosity had been satisfied and Mr. and Mrs. Gaffney were not the least bit suspicious about anything. Grampa was now happy and well occupied. He even seemed to take pride in his appearance once more. He was careful now to wear clean clothes—ones without rips or holes. And he was enjoying writing his book with Tallulah's help. She was a bit bizarre, but she certainly was competent.

When Sibyl gave the bread basket back to her brother, she noticed that Mark was grinning. Everything was fine, just fine. So she grinned again too!

Seven

PROBLEMS

The weeks that followed were happy and productive ones for Grampa Will and Tallulah. Together they had written one third of the book, and both were satisfied with what they had accomplished so far.

The children saw little of their grandfather during those early weeks of spring. They saw even less of Tallulah, who was usually gone by the time Mark and Sibyl returned from school. Jeremy was allowed few glimpses of Grampa's new friend because Sibyl was worried that he would become too intrigued by the friendly ghost. Tallulah was concerned about frightening the "dear little child."

Occasionally, Grampa would have dinner with the family at the Big House. Once in a while, Mr. Gaffney would go over to play cards with him. Grampa still went to church every Sunday and even found time to visit the elderly Ledbetters down the street now and then. It was now obvious to everybody that Grampa Will had never been more content since coming to Lincoln.

"I don't believe he's grieving for Nana Rosa as much as he used to," Mrs. Gaffney noted. "He's making a new life for himself and doing quite well."

"Writing that book has certainly been therapeutic," Mr. Gaffney observed. "And, I might add, he's done remarkably well without a ghostwriter." He cast a meaningful glance at his two oldest children as he said this. "I've read the first few chapters of the book and they're well written. I really think Dad will have a good chance of selling it."

Mark and Sibyl exchanged a knowing glance. They knew the reason for Grampa's newfound contentment and for his unexpected power with a pen: Tallulah Farquar! She had brightened Grampa's lonely days and provided the needed inspiration for the book.

Although she still called Grampa everything from Wilfred to Winthrop, the kids had to admit that her spelling was faultless. Their grandfather had boasted just the other day that Tallulah had written the words *hippopotamus* and *rhinoceros* without having to look them up in a dictionary!

Sibyl and Mark were happy for Grampa Will. But they were also a bit worried. What would happen when the book was completed and Tallulah's services were no longer needed? Their grandfather was growing more and more attached to his phantom friend. He even asked her to come back in the evenings sometimes so they could simply visit together. The youngsters didn't always see her while they were spending time with Grampa Will, but they could always tell when Tallulah was around.

Sometimes they would see Grampa's empty coffee mug float through the air into the kitchen. Then it would return, more slowly this time and filled to the rim. Sometimes the papers on Grampa Will's desk seemed to be shuffling themselves into neat little piles. And once, when Mrs. Gaffney had sent Sibyl over to collect Grampa's dirty laundry, clothes, bed sheets, and towels flew through the air and collapsed into the large wicker basket.

"Thanks, Tallulah," Sibyl had said to the invisible ghost.

"You're welcome, Mabel," came her voice out of thin air.

Most of the time Tallulah had no idea that she had "turned herself off" as Mark called it. She would simply fade from view, due to her lack of concentration on remaining visible. Sometimes she would disappear on purpose and then forget to make herself visible again.

Like the time Mrs. Gaffney came over to talk to Grampa about spring cleaning. Tallulah had quickly dropped her pen and writing tablet and "turned herself off." She was so quiet and so still, even after Mrs. Gaffney had gone, that Grampa Will had begun to wonder if she'd gone home. But Tallulah had simply fallen asleep on the sofa instead!

One evening Mr. Gaffney had come over unannounced with his friend Harve Hurley. They'd asked if Grampa was interested in a few hands of gin rummy. Tallulah had been invisibly enjoying a John Wayne movie on television.

Of all the modern wonders in Grampa's home, the television was the one that fascinated Tallulah the most—besides the microwave of course. She found the game shows and the commercials too loud and lively for her liking, and the afternoon soap operas always embarrassed her. But Tallulah did enjoy the religious programs and the old movies, especially the John Wayne films. Grampa often turned the set on as a special treat for the appreciative ghost. She would sit primly on the sofa, entranced by the quick-moving images on the screen and completely enjoying herself.

"There's no one watching this," Mr. Gaffney had said that evening. He had walked over to the television set and turned it off. He'd been totally unaware of the female phantom who sat on the sofa bristling with anger. "No use wasting electricity," he'd added.

And as if that wasn't bad enough, Mr. Hurley had then plopped himself down on the very end of the sofa that Tallulah'd been occupying! He was a large, heavyset man and Tallulah feared she would be crushed. The frightened ghost almost shrieked out loud as she flew up off the couch. She had exerted such a burst of energy that later she claimed she had been exhausted for days afterward.

"I feel a bit of a draft in here, don't you?" Mr. Gaffney had asked his father.

"Well, why don't we play cards in the kitchen," Grampa'd suggested.

As the men had made their way into the other room, Tallulah had leaned against Grampa's desk. She'd tried to catch her breath again. She'd been annoyed that her movie had been interrupted and that she'd nearly been sat on by a rude stranger.

For one brief moment, she'd considered making herself visible. She would put on her most horrifying expression and scare the wits out of the two visitors, Tallulah had decided! But before she had made any definite plans, Grampa Will had returned to the living room and clicked the TV back on.

"Turn it off when your movie is over," he'd said, looking around the room for a hint of Tallulah's presence. "I'll see you in the morning, Tallulah. Good night."

"Good night, Wilfred," Tallulah'd whispered back. "And thank you." She'd settled herself comfortably on the couch. How was it possible, she'd wondered, that such a kind and thoughtful gentleman could have such a rude, thoughtless son?

Eight

SOLUTIONS!

Everything had been going smoothly. Mark and Sibyl could not imagine any problems cropping up. So on the following Saturday afternoon they were more than a little surprised to hear someone crying as they arrived at Grampa Will's. It sounded like Tallulah! Something was terribly wrong!

Sibyl glanced anxiously at Mark. She then quickly led the way into the kitchen where they found the ghost sobbing at the table. Grampa Will looked worried and slightly confused. He was trying to comfort Tallulah.

"Come now, Tallulah! Stop your crying. We'll work out something, you can count on that. No more crying now. You'll make yourself . . . er . . . sick."

"What's the matter?" Mark asked. He was almost afraid to know.

"Tallulah's house has been sold," Grampa said. "The new family moved in yesterday."

"Complete with four children, one St. Bernard dog, and three Siamese cats!" Tallulah wailed. She reached for a dish towel and used it to blow her nose and to wipe her streaming eyes. "Where can I go now? Oh, what will become of me?"

"Why don't you just scare the new family away?" Mark suggested. "A big family with all those pets and kids won't want to stay in a haunted house for long."

"I simply don't feel very frightening, Martin," Tallulah confessed with a dispirited moan.

"Mark—the name is Mark," the boy corrected her.

"You aren't very frightening at all!" Grampa Will declared. "Why, anybody could take one look at you and know that you're a friendly ghost."

"The friendliest!" Sibyl added with a warm smile.

"We'll just have to find you another place to live," Grampa Will said. Mark and Sibyl agreed. "There will be no more book writing until you are comfortably settled someplace."

"Thank you so much." Tallulah sniffed gratefully. "I've had to hide myself away in the cellar. It's dingy, dark, and dreadful down there! It smells! It's not homey at all."

"I didn't think ghosts were bothered by that kind of stuff," Sibyl said.

"Well, I do not suffer from the heat and cold as I did when I was . . . er . . . human," Tallulah admitted. "But I am sensitive to some discomforts. It's not a good thing for ghosts to reside where there are animals," she went on. "They always know you are around—even when you're invisible. They bark and bristle and make quite a commotion. That St. Bernard monster is a blustering nuisance, don't you know!"

"I guess you can't move in with us then." Sibyl sighed. "We have Hoodwink, and he . . . er . . . doesn't like ghosts either."

"Oh, no!" Tallulah exclaimed. "Cats are even more sensitive and bothersome than dogs. They hiss and snarl so! And they stalk you like prey."

"That's too bad," Grampa put in. "My son's house has a nice big attic—airy and roomy. It would be a perfect place for you."

"I think not." Tallulah sighed. "I could not feel at all comfortable with that big orange cat hissing after me all the time."

"Will you go back to your old place tonight?" Mark asked.

"I'd rather not," Tallulah replied. "That dog makes my nerves jittery. Last night I had to sleep curled up on the top of the laundry washing box . . . er . . . washing machine. That animal put his enormous feet on the top of it and peered at me. He barked and growled all the while. It was most disturbing!"

"Well, you'll *have* to stay at our house then," Mark said. "We'll leave Hoodwink out at night, and you can have the whole attic to yourself."

"That's what you'll have to do, Tallulah, until we can make other arrangements," Grampa Will agreed.

So Tallulah, reluctant but relieved, invisibly

followed Mark and Sibyl to the Big House later that evening. They took her quickly to the attic and wished her a heartfelt good night. Hoodwink, who usually slept at the foot of Sibyl's bed, found himself shoved out the back door just when he was ready to settle down for the night.

"Sorry, Hoodwink," Sibyl apologized.

The next morning after Sibyl and Mark had left for school, Grampa Will came over to the Big House and asked Mrs. Gaffney if Jeremy could go to the park. Grampa promised to push Jeremy on the swings after they had gone on a long walk around the block. The little boy happily agreed. He enjoyed the cheerful chirping of the birds and admired the new blooms on the redbud trees. He had no idea at all that Grampa Will was scouting out a suitable home for the shiny-water lady.

But it was no use! All of the homes with *For Sale* signs out front were still occupied. Nor were they suitable for a solitary ghost. With a heavy heart and extremely tired feet, Grampa Will returned Jeremy to his mother. He made his way to his small cottage and eased himself into his favorite chair. Grampa sighed with disappointment.

Tallulah had been watching a John Wayne movie, but without her usual enthusiasm. She gently removed her tired friend's jacket and hung it in the closet. Grampa was still sitting in his chair staring glumly out the window when Sibyl and Mark came in later that afternoon.

"You're home early, aren't you?" Grampa Will asked, glancing at his watch.

"We got out an hour early," Mark explained. "And next week we don't go to school at all. It's spring break."

"Grumpff!" was Grampa's only response.

"Mark and I will have a whole week off from school," Sibyl said to Tallulah. "We can help find you a new house."

"That's what dear Winfield has been doing all morning, but to no avail," Tallulah said with a sigh.

"There must be one empty house in Lincoln that's just right for you," Sibyl said optimistically. She perched herself on the arm of her grandfather's chair. Glancing at her brother, she saw him frown at the sad expression on Tallulah's shimmering face. Even her ringlets seemed to sag.

"If we don't find you a place here in town, we're sure to find an empty farmhouse out in the country somewhere," Mark added.

"I think there's one on the road to Elkhart, isn't there?" Sibyl asked her grandfather.

"Grumpff!" came his response.

"It won't do, Sylvia," Tallulah spoke up. "It's too far away, don't you know."

Sibyl shrugged. This time she didn't even care that Tallulah had called her by the wrong name—again.

"Does it really matter how far the house is from here?" Mark asked. "I mean, you can fly or . . . or float . . . or whatever it is that ghosts do," he stammered.

"But moving about takes more concentration than making oneself visible," Tallulah explained. "And I'm not as spry as I used to be."

"I wouldn't ask you to do all that flitting around," Grampa Will said gruffly. "We'll just have to make other arrangements."

"I'll do whatever you think best, Woodley," Tallulah answered meekly.

"Grumpff!" Grampa Will replied. Sibyl and Mark tried not to giggle. Woodley, indeed!

The next week was hectic with house hunting. Sibyl attached Jeremy's bike seat to the back of her ten-speed and pedaled all over town looking for a suitable residence for Tallulah.

Sibyl never realized how difficult finding just the right home could be. "I thought anything would do for a ghost—even an old closet," she confided to her brother. Mark nodded understandingly. He spent a lot of time reading the *House for Sale* ads in the newspaper, but he wasn't having any luck either.

Tallulah couldn't go on living in the attic much longer. Hoodwink was becoming crankier and more suspicious every day. Grampa and Tallulah agreed not to do any more writing until a new home had been found. "Writer's block,"

Grampa complained when his son asked him how the book was coming along.

"Spring fever," Mr. Gaffney insisted.

Tallulah did not go out at all in search of new living quarters. "My nerves are shattered, don't you know." Instead, she planted herself in front of Grampa Will's television and watched old movies the entire week long.

Once when Grampa was out on a scouting expedition, Mrs. Gaffney came over with a basket of clean towels and bed sheets. She had set the clothes basket just inside the front door and was about to leave when she noticed then that the television was on. Stepping inside, she walked across the room and turned off the TV.

Tallulah was not about to miss a single minute of this exciting adventure film featuring an enormous ape with an impossible fascination for a lovely young woman. The ghost quickly got up from the sofa and turned the TV back on. Mrs. Gaffney stared at the television set as if it had come alive and turned it off again.

This time Tallulah waited impatiently until the intruder left the house before turning the movie back on. But in less than fifteen minutes Mrs. Gaffney returned, carrying a plate full of fresh muffins and two pairs of neatly pressed trousers.

"I'm sure I turned that thing off before I left," she murmured as she stared at the TV screen. She carried Grampa's trousers to his bedroom and then came back into the living room to place the muffins on the desk and again turn off the TV.

No sooner had she stepped out the front door when Tallulah turned the television back on. Mrs. Gaffney heard the unmistakable sound of King Kong's horrendous roar and popped back in through the door. "Strange, very strange!" she said, shaking her head as she flicked the TV off once again.

Tallulah was getting annoyed. She was sorely tempted to pull Mrs. Gaffney's hair or hit her with a sofa pillow. Fortunately, she resisted these urges and waited until she saw the woman enter the back door of her own house before turning the television on once more. She hoped it would be the last time.

"It was quite exasperating, don't you know," she told Grampa later. He chuckled, imagining his daughter-in-law's battle with the television set.

"Yes, Barb spoke to me about it," he told Tallulah with a grin. "She said it was the strangest thing. She'd click off the TV and it would click back on again! I told her I thought there was a short somewhere."

"A short what?" Tallulah wanted to know. She drew herself up to her full height and pushed back a wayward curl.

"Er . . . never you mind," Grampa told her.

"Grumpff!" Tallulah snorted.

"You needn't be worrying yourself about my daughter-in-law. You have more important things to think about now," Grampa continued with a knowing smile.

When Tallulah turned questioning eyes upon him, he blurted out, "I've found you a wonderful place to live!"

Nine

A HOME FOR TALLULAH

"I'll be taking Tallulah to her new home tomorrow—at the Ledbetters," Grampa Will said. He poked his head into the bathroom where Mark was keeping an eye on Jeremy. The little boy was in the tub surrounded by a small fleet of colorful plastic boats.

"The Ledbetters!" Mark exclaimed. He raised his eyebrows in surprise. "Are they moving?"

"No," Grampa said, looking quite pleased with himself. "They are not moving."

"Then how come—" Mark began. He stopped abruptly when he saw his grandfather's warning frown. The man tilted his head in Jeremy's direction. The little boy was looking inquiringly from one to the other.

Mark thought he would die of curiosity. He wanted to hear all about everything, but he knew they couldn't speak about Tallulah in front of Jeremy. Just then his mother came up the stairs.

"I've come to rescue Jeremy before he turns completely pruney," she said with a smile.

"Look, Grampa!" the little boy called out as he

held up a small foot. "I have wrinkles too!" His mother pulled him from the tub, wrapped him in a large bath towel, and marched him down the hall.

"I'll clean up in here," Mark called after his mother. Then he turned quickly to his grandfather. "I want to go with you tomorrow," he said, lowering his voice. "I know Sib will want to go to. May we come along?"

Grampa Will said that they could.

It was nearly two o'clock the following afternoon when Mark arrived at his grandfather's. He had brought a sleepy-eyed Jeremy along. "Mom had to run some errands," he explained. "I woke Jeremy up from his nap to bring him with us."

"But where's your sister?" Grampa Will asked. He glanced over Mark's shoulder.

"She had to baby-sit for the Coopers," Mark said with a grin. "She tried to get out of it, but couldn't find anybody to fill in for her." He cast a brief glance around the cottage. "Are we *all* ready to go?" he asked, wondering just where Tallulah was.

"We're *all* ready," Grampa Will replied with a knowing wink. He started down the sidewalk in the direction of the Ledbetter house. "I was just telling *our friend* about Mr. and Mrs. Ledbetter before you came over," Grampa said.

Mark only nodded. He was still wondering where Tallulah was. He saw no telltale sign of her presence. He guessed that she was refusing to show herself because of Jeremy.

"The house is a huge, old rambling place," Grampa Will went on. "There's a nice attic on the third floor and several large bedrooms on the second. The Ledbetters don't use that part of the house anymore, or so they tell me. Too many stairs. And they have no pets," he added.

"But will they mind company?" Mark asked. He glanced sidelong at his grandfather and raised his eyebrows significantly.

"Why should they?" Grampa Will asked. "They won't *know* they have company. They are two elderly people who stay in their dayroom off the kitchen most of the time. They sleep in the downstairs bedroom."

"Their house *is* awfully big," Mark replied. He'd been there once or twice before with his grandfather. Although he had not taken the liberty of wandering all over the house, Mark could tell that it was roomy. In fact, it was a lot like the Gaffneys' house. The perfect place for a friendly ghost! "I guess it's big enough that no one will be bumping into each other," he said.

An indignant cough could be heard coming out of thin air. Grampa Will grinned broadly. "I doubt there will be any of that," he said.

As the three Gaffneys and their invisible companion approached the large, grayish-white house with its faded green shutters, Grampa Will raised a hand in greeting. "Good afternoon, Elwyn. How are you today, Opal?"

The elderly couple, who were even older than Grampa Will, sat rocking lazily on the front porch. "Hey, Will! Who's that you've got with you?" Elwyn Ledbetter asked in a croaking voice. He squinted his eyes trying to get a better glimpse of Mark and Jeremy.

"Brought my grandsons along," Grampa Will bellowed out. "You remember Mark, don't you, and little Jeremy?"

"I'm not little!" Jeremy protested, clinging to his brother's hand and frowning sleepily.

"Why, of course you're not!" Opal Ledbetter sympathized. She reached out a small, wrinkled hand toward the little boy who reluctantly made his way up the porch steps. "Would you like a cookie?" she asked kindly. Jeremy nodded. Mark, who was also fond of cookies, hoped she'd offer him one too.

"Let's all go into the house, then," Mrs. Ledbetter said hospitably. "We can all have some cookies."

Grampa exchanged smiles with Mark, and the three of them followed the Ledbetters into the house. They stayed for an hour, sitting around the kitchen table, eating sugar cookies and chatting. It was apparent that Mr. and Mrs. Ledbetter were quite pleased to have company. Grampa seemed pleased about something too.

Jeremy was content to stand beside Mrs. Ledbetter's chair and eat one cookie after another. But Mark began to worry. He wondered where Tallulah was now. Was she making her way from room to room? Would she decide that living with the Ledbetters would suit her? Or had she left already, displeased with the arrangements?

"Grampa says you have a big upstairs, but you never play there," Jeremy mumbled, his mouth full of cookie.

Mark was startled, but the Ledbetters simply laughed. "Me and Opal don't do much playing anywhere anymore," Elwyn Ledbetter replied. His wife chuckled. So did Grampa Will. Mark forced a laugh too, but Jeremy widened his eyes in surprise.

"Don't you even play hide-and-seek?" he asked.

"No, not even that," their elderly hostess replied with a sweet smile.

"We could play now," Jeremy suggested. "And I'll be it."

"Maybe some other time," Grampa intervened. He rose to his feet. "We've got to be going now."

"So soon?" Opal asked, glancing at Jeremy in a sad-to-see-you-go sort of way. "You be sure to stop in again sometime soon. And bring these handsome fellows with you."

Grampa Will assured her that he would. Mark remembered his manners and thanked Mrs. Ledbetter for the cookies and lemonade. He then hoisted Jeremy onto his back. "How about a horsey ride?" he asked.

"Yeah, giddyup!" Jeremy replied brightly. "C'mon, horsey!" Mark galloped out of the kitchen, through the living room, and out the front door. Jeremy giggled with pleasure and clung tightly to his brother's neck.

Mark was halfway down the sidewalk before he turned to look back. He saw Grampa wave good-bye to the elderly couple on the porch before following Mark and Jeremy down the street. Grampa's lips were moving, and Mark thought at first that his grandfather was talking to himself. Then he realized that his grandfather was discussing the new living arrangements with an invisible Tallulah. Mark smiled knowingly.

"Giddyup to Grampa," Jeremy ordered, so Mark turned around again and galloped back toward Grampa Will.

"Ride 'em cowboy!" Grampa called out. "I'll see you back at my place," he added for Mark's benefit. Mark nodded. Then panting a little, he galloped home with Jeremy clinging to his back and kicking him in the ribs.

Mark hung around in the backyard waiting for Tallulah and Grampa Will to return. He was eager to hear what had been decided. So he was quite disappointed when his grandfather emerged from around the corner of the house and gave him a dismissive wave of his hand. "I'll talk with you later," he said curtly.

If Mark was feeling impatient and curious, so was Sibyl. When she rode up into the yard on her bike a short time later, she could hardly wait to pull her older brother aside. "So how did it go?" she demanded. She cast a cautious glance in the direction of the kitchen where her mother and Jeremy were making a salad together.

"I don't know," Mark said with an impatient shrug. "I was keeping an eye on Jeremy all afternoon while Mom was gone and Grampa didn't want me to come over."

"*I'm* going over there right this minute!" Sibyl declared. "I can't stand the suspense any longer." She quietly slipped out the front door and around to the back of the house. Mark followed her eagerly.

Grampa Will answered their urgent knock with a smile and a chuckle. "She likes it!" was all he said. But his comment answered the unasked question on their faces.

"That's great!" Sibyl declared. Now Tallulah would have a comfortable home of her own and Hoodwink wouldn't have to sleep outside any longer.

"I'm glad," Mark put in. He raised his hand to greet the shimmering apparition on the sofa.

"I, too, am quite pleased," Tallulah said. She rose like a mist from the couch. "I was just leaving now. I must move in and get settled."

"Move in?" Sibyl asked. "Get settled? What do you mean? You don't have any furniture or clothes or anything."

"You won't mind living with the Ledbetters?" Mark asked before Tallulah could answer his sister's question.

"Why, no indeed!" Tallulah replied. "To be sure, their home is quite dusty, but I'll have the entire second and third floors to myself." Her ghostly face beamed with pleasure. "I believe I'll take the poor dears under my wing."

Grampa laughed heartily. "Opal and Elwyn are mighty lucky, that's all I can say!" he declared with a smile.

"Lucky?" Mark asked. A puzzled frown creased his brow. "Why do you say that? They won't even know Tallulah is around."

"That doesn't matter," Grampa Will said. "Their lives will improve a bit every day—just as mine did. Tallulah will see to that."

Mark's frown deepened, but Sibyl's face lit up. "I get it!" she declared excitedly. "Do you remember the story about the shoemaker and the elves?" She asked Mark. "The little elves kept doing nice things for the shoemaker. He had no idea who it was—at first."

Mark smiled and nodded his head. "Now I know what you mean about being lucky," he said to Grampa Will. "I think you're right. And the Ledbetters won't have a dusty house for long!"

"What's this about a shoemaker and some elves?" Tallulah asked. she looked from one Gaffney to another so quickly that her sausage curls swirled around her face.

"It's a fairy tale," Grampa Will told her. "I'm surprised you haven't read it."

"I certainly will do so, if you suggest it, Wilmot," Tallulah said amiably. "Now I must go along. So much to do, don't you know."

"Wait, Tallulah!" Sibyl called out. "You are coming back, aren't you? I mean you will continue to help Grampa with his book, won't you?"

"Of course!" Tallulah declared. She seemed mildly astonished that Sibyl would think otherwise. "We Farquars have never been quitters!" she added proudly. "Besides, your grandfather has another book to begin immediately after this one, don't you know."

At their surprised expressions, she turned to Grampa Will. "Didn't you tell the children about your second book, Woodrow?"

"Not yet," he replied with an amused grin. Looking from Sibyl to Mark, he said, "Tallulah thinks that I could write about my war experiences on the Solomon Islands. It might make a good novel—a men's adventure story."

"What a great idea!" Mark exclaimed. He beamed with approval. An idea struck him then, and he turned his happy gaze upon Tallulah. "Say, speaking of war stories, could you help me with a report on the Civil War, Tallulah? I mean, the War Between the States," he amended for her benefit.

"Why, certainly, Melvin! I'd be most happy to, but not just at the moment. I must go. There's so very much to do, don't you know?" and she disappeared with a final swish of her long skirts.

"I want to have a word with your father," Grampa Will said, breaking the contented silence that followed Tallulah's disappearance. "I'm ready for him to find me a typist. I've got over two hundred pages written." He indicated the stack of yellow paper on the desk.

Sibyl giggled then. "I bet there won't be a single spelling mistake."

"Yeah, but we might not recognize the author's name," Mark added with a laugh. "Tallulah is *not* good with names."

They all laughed together, and Grampa laughed loudest of all. They were enjoying the excitement of their shared secret.

"Who'd have thought that we'd be friends with a ghost?" Mark exclaimed when he'd caught his breath again. "I mean a *real* ghost!"

"And one that spells!" Grampa Will reminded him with a wink. "I daresay that ghosts are a dime a dozen, but one that can spell is really a treasure."

"Treasure!" Sibyl repeated gaily. She then began to spell the word, mimicking Tallulah's tone. "T-r-e-a-s-u-r-e! Treasure!"

THE MAGIC CONTINUES... WITH
LYNNE REID BANKS

THE SECRET OF THE INDIAN
71040-4/$3.99 U.S.

THE INDIAN IN THE CUPBOARD
60012-9/$3.99 U.S./$4.99 Can.

THE RETURN OF THE INDIAN
70284-3/$3.99 U.S.

I, HOUDINI 70649-0/$3.99 U.S.

THE FAIRY REBEL 70650-4/$3.99 U.S.

THE FARTHEST-AWAY MOUNTAIN
71303-9/$3.99 U.S.

ONE MORE RIVER 71563-5/$3.99 U.S.

THE ADVENTURES OF KING MIDAS
71564-3/$3.99 U.S.

Buy these books at your local bookstore or use this coupon for ordering:

Mail to: Avon Books, Dept BP, Box 767, Rte 2, Dresden, TN 38225 C
Please send me the book(s) I have checked above.
❏ My check or money order— no cash or CODs please— for $______________is enclosed (please add $1.50 to cover postage and handling for each book ordered— Canadian residents add 7% GST).
❏ Charge my VISA/MC Acct#______________________Exp Date______________
Minimum credit card order is two books or $6.00 (please add postage and handling charge of $1.50 per book — Canadian residents add 7% GST). For faster service, call 1-800-762-0779. Residents of Tennessee, please call 1-800-633-1607. Prices and numbers are subject to change without notice. Please allow six to eight weeks for delivery.

Name______________________________________
Address____________________________________
City___________________State/Zip______________
Telephone No.______________________

LRB 1093

Celebrati... ...y Kids!

CAMELOT presents

BEVERLY CLEARY FAVORITES!

☐ **HENRY HUGGINS**
70912-0 ($3.99 US/$4.99 Can)

☐ **HENRY AND BEEZUS**
70914-7 ($3.99 US/$4.99 Can)

☐ **HENRY AND THE CLUBHOUSE**
70915-5

☐ **ELLEN**
70913

☐ **HENR**
7091

☐ **BEE**
7091

☐ **RAM**
7091

☐ **MIT**
7092

☐ **RUN**
7095

☐ **RAM**
7095

☐ **RIB**
7095

☐ **STRIDER**
71236-9 ($3.99 US/$4.99 Can)

☐ **HENRY AND THE PAPER ROUTE**
70921-X ($3.99 US/$4.99 Can)

☐ **RAMONA AND HER MOTHER**
...an)

Buy these

Mail to: A
Please se
☐ My che
(please a
add 7% G
☐ Charge
Minimum
$1.50 p
1-800-762
are subje

Name
Address
City_______________State/Zip_______________
Telephone No.________________

BEV 1293